AFFILIATE MARKETING

How To Make Money Online And Build Your Own $100,000+ Affiliate Marketing Online Business

Table of Contents

Introduction

Thank you for taking the time to download this book, Affiliate Marketing: How To Make Money Online And Build Your Own $100,000 Affiliate Marketing Online Business!

This book covers the different topics associated with affiliate marketing, starting with its definition, trends, opportunities, and current options, and will teach you various strategies and techniques to become successful in affiliate marketing.

At the completion of this book you will have a good understanding of the affiliate marketing industry and what it offers to the entrepreneur, and be able to apply the techniques presented to your own online business enterprise.

Once again, thanks for downloading this book, I hope you find it to be helpful!

Chapter One: What Is Affiliate Marketing?

The concept of affiliate marketing as an online business intricately connects to the robust expansion of Web-based consumer shopping trends of the last couple of decades. E-commerce and online shopping have exploded in growth spurred on by the accessibility of high-speed Internet access, Web-enabled smartphones and mobile devices, and increasingly busy schedules that have caused consumers to look for faster, more practical ways to search for products and purchase them at the most convenient times, regardless of physical location.

E-commerce pervades much of modern life, with nearly all conceivable consumer goods and services available for online purchase. The average consumer can access his computer, tablet, or smartphone and shop online for anything he or she needs. Clothes, furniture, toys, books, music, movies, hotel rooms, airline tickets, fitness equipment, vitamin supplements, electronics, music lessons, and more without having to leave his office desk, kitchen table, or bed. Products and services are delivered right to the consumer's doorstep, or in many cases may be available for pick-up at the retailer's local distribution center, saving time and costs.

The concept of online shopping was first explored sometime in the early 1970's, when the ARPANET, one of the earliest versions of the

World Wide Web, was utilized by students at the Stanford Artificial Intelligence Laboratory and the Massachusetts Institute of Technology to initiate a cannabis transaction. In 1979, Michael Aldrich proposed a demonstration of the very first online shopping system. By 1981, Thomson Holidays UK had installed a fully operational business-to-business online shopping system.

In 1982, France Telecom introduced Minitel for online ordering. By 1984, the online home shopping revolution began when Gateshead SIS/Tesco launched the very first business-to-consumer online shopping system. A 72-year-old online home shopper, Mrs. Jane Snowball, was the very first online home shopper, using the Videotex computer technology to order groceries from her television remote control and have them delivered to her local Tesco grocery store, which then delivered the items to her doorstep.

It was Aldrich's technology used for this online shopping system. Speaking to the BBC, Aldrich related that what they did was to turn a home television set into a computer terminal. "That was the big leap."

Kevin Turner, a principal lecturer at Brighton Business School, described Aldrich and his company as way advanced for their time. "It demonstrated that people could do transactions from home."

This first online home shopping system was initially designed to aid pensioners who had problems with mobility and would benefit from being able to order essential groceries and other products from their home. Three UK-based retailers, namely Tesco, Greggs, and Lloyds Pharmacy, took part in the experiment. Although Bradford Council later adopted the system, it never became widely used, at least not until the advent of home computers and Internet access.

Compuserve launched the first Electronic Mall in North America in April 1984. In May 1989, the first Web-based e-commerce system was introduced by Sequoia Data Corporation, called Compumarket. In this platform, sellers could post assorted items for sale, and buyers could browse the site and initiate transactions using their credit card. By the early to mid-1990's, commercial websites selling books, software, and other items were being launched online.

1995 was a notable year for e-commerce, with Jeff Bezos launching Amazon.com, and Pierre Omidyar founding eBay (then known as AuctionWeb). Today, Amazon and eBay are major players in the e-commerce sector. By 2015, Amazon.com accounted for almost half of all e-commerce growth, driven by the steady growth of its Prime membership accounts. By 2020, it is estimated that up to 50% of all households in the United States will have an Amazon Prime membership.

As an Internet concept, affiliate marketing was first introduced by William J. Tobin, founder of PC Flowers and Gifts. The service was introduced on the Prodigy Network in 1989 and continued until 1996, generating sales of over $6 million yearly on the Prodigy platform. PC Flowers and Gifts pioneered the concept of paying a commission on sales to the larger network (Prodigy), thereby introducing the affiliate marketing concept.

Simply defined, affiliate marketing is the process of generating a commission through the promotion of another company's products and/or services. An affiliate marketer will search for products or services, promote these products and services to his audience, and earn a part of the profit for every sale made.

Affiliate marketing involves four tiers in the process, namely, the merchant or retailer; the network, which holds the product offers for affiliates to select and handles transactions; a publisher or affiliate; and the customer purchasing the products. As affiliate marketing has evolved and become a substantial segment of the overall e-commerce market, it has spawned other entities which are also involved in the process, such as third-party vendors, affiliate management agencies, and super-affiliates.

For the merchant or retailer, affiliate marketing is an efficient and convenient way to increase awareness and sales. A business owner can offer its own affiliate program with a performance-based structure that rewards a commission fee for every generated lead or sale, with the primary target of tapping markets which would otherwise not be reached by your primary website.

In the world of affiliate marketing, the party that creates the product or service being marketed is known as the merchant. The merchant may also be referred to as the seller, brand, creator, retailer, or vendor, whichever term is most appropriate. Merchants can be huge companies, mid-sized enterprises, or smaller entrepreneurs.

Meanwhile, the affiliate or the publisher can also be a single individual, a medium-sized enterprise, or a large company. It is the affiliate's role to spearhead the marketing efforts, promoting the affiliated products and services to a wide range of audiences using a host of techniques and strategies. Over the years, the methods employed in affiliate marketing have included review blogs or sites, YouTube channels, e-zines, and other strategies.

The intermediary between the merchant and the affiliate is known as the network. The affiliate network handles the payment and product delivery portions of the process. Some merchants also to choose to only work with affiliate networks, meaning potential affiliates must go through their selected network to be able to promote any products or services. Most affiliate networks also offer a database from which affiliate marketers can choose which ones to promote.

In this e-Book, we will focus more on the affiliate or publisher side of the affiliate marketing industry. What are the steps you will need to take to become an affiliate marketer and make money off promoting other products or services on your own marketing channels? What opportunities are available so you can be a part of this potentially lucrative enterprise? We will look at the possibilities so you will have a better understanding of just how this can help you earn profitable rewards down the road.

First, let us look at the first steps you need to take to become an online affiliate marketer.

Chapter Summary

- Online affiliate marketing has grown exponentially with the advent of e-commerce, online shopping, and mobile data.

- Affiliate marketing refers to the promotion of another company's products or services, and earning a commission from the process.

- Affiliates may be individuals, small or medium enterprises, or large firms.

Chapter Two: How To Become An Affiliate Marketer

Affiliate marketing has often been cited as a source of passive income. While it is true that many affiliate marketers have become successful and are now reaping the rewards of passive earnings from their affiliate marketing businesses, a lot of work had to be put in first. There is no overnight formula of success for this industry, so you will need to start with the basics.

In his article "Four Myths About Affiliate Marketing" published on July 8, 2014, *Forbes.com* contributor Steve Olenski, who is also a content marketing influencer and member of the Editorial Board of the Journal of Digital and Social Media Marketing, explains that in an affiliate marketing program, you need to invest a lot of work, but often you are entering a market where there is already a lot of competition, which means you will not be bringing in money right away. Olenski says many business owners and entrepreneurs think that all they have to do is set up a site and select an affiliate to work with, and the whole thing will just play out. But a 2013 study made by Three Ladders Marketing reveals that only 0.6% of affiliate marketers remained for more than a year, which highlights the fact that affiliate marketing requires time and effort in order to become profitable eventually.

Online affiliate marketing requires the same commitment, perseverance, and dedication much like any other business venture. Randy Duermyer of *TheBalance.com* notes, "Can you make money with affiliate marketing? The short answer is yes; affiliate programs can earn extra money and even a full-time income from home." However, Duermeyer points out, it is a lot more complicated than most people are aware of. In fact, just like any other business enterprise or home venture, becoming successful in online affiliate marketing depends a lot on whether you, as the entrepreneur, accurately and consistently stick to steps that are part of the overall process, and not just focus on making money right away.

Duermyer also points out that the problem with affiliate marketing, just like other home business opportunities, is the prevalence of get-rich-quick programs and deceptive "experts" who make it seem that affiliate marketing gets results quickly and requires little effort. As it is, the truth about affiliate marketing is not very different from other work-at-home enterprises; some people make it big, some others meet moderate success and meet their goals, while others don't even profit at all. More important than finding out whether affiliate marketing will make money is figuring out if it is right for you.

The very first thing to think about when planning your affiliate marketing business is your niche or market. You would want to start with a niche, category, or market which you are already familiar or passionate about because you will need to build an online presence around this niche and market it to your target audience. If you choose a niche you are not personally familiar about, how can you effectively communicate its selling points to your audience?

What topics or interests are you already very passionate about in your daily life? It would be helpful to come up with a list so you can narrow down your choices. Your niche may be anywhere from health and fitness, home furnishings, clothes, accessories, pets, toys, books, music, organic food, shoes, electronics, car accessories, household cleaning materials, movies, meditation, home improvement, etc.

Once you have a list of potential niches or categories, you can then go through the list and research which ones you can focus on. As an example, if you already practice yoga two or three times a week, you may decide that your affiliate marketing efforts would revolve around promoting yoga-related products, classes, and instructional materials. Because you are already very familiar with the subject, you will have an easier time coming up with promotional ideas for your online channels, and you likely will also have existing networks or contacts that can help with getting the affiliate marketing off the ground.

You will also need to consider whether this potential niche or topic can be lucrative in the marketing sense. A lot of times, what topics you are passionate about may take a backseat to other potential niches which you may not necessarily be interested in personally but can be much more profitable depending on your location, target audience, and other factors. For instance, you may be very passionate about online harmonica lessons and would want to revolve your online affiliate marketing efforts around this topic, but after careful research and analysis, you realize that a more popular niche such as bed and bath accessories can be more profitable overall.

The good thing about this is you can always learn, educate yourself, and become more equipped to handle a topic or niche which you may not be as familiar about. In this age of information and easy access to many various sources of learning, you can opt for a topic which is more lucrative in the marketing sense and choose to familiarize yourself over time, thereby adding to your knowledge while also catering to what the market demands.

Still, if you do find that one or more of the topics or categories you are already passionate about or familiar with can become financially viable for affiliate marketing, it would be better to stick to these interests. Keep in mind that affiliate marketing would involve a lot of writing and content production revolving around the topic or topics you eventually select, and it is undoubtedly much easier to produce content around topics you already care about personally rather than a niche you are still learning about.

Forbes.com's Olenski adds in his article that many companies do not even consider trying an affiliate marketing program because they believe their market is very small. Some companies will attempt to enter into much larger niches despite not having any interest in that particular niche. While it may be true that the more popular niches do better with affiliate marketing, this does not mean the smaller niches are doomed to fail. What is important, Olenski says, is to keep focused on your goals and your company's mission, while partnering with affiliates who know how to make you relevant in your market.

The online audience you will be targeting has a lot of options to choose from, and it is imperative to sound like an authority on the subject you choose. This means creating content that is in-depth, relatable, and without sounding contrived or forced. High-caliber content is the lifeblood of affiliate marketing, so you would want to find a niche that is ultimately interesting for you, and easier to convey positively to your target market.

You will also need to consider whether there is room for another affiliate marketer in this category or niche. If a particular category is popular, chances are there are already affiliate marketers for it, and you will need to weigh whether there is room for you to join and still be lucrative. This also takes into consideration factors such as target audience and geographic location; for instance, even if there are already many affiliate marketers for a certain product, you may be the only one targeting a specific region or city, in which case you can still potentially bring in lots of revenue.

After you have decided what niche or category you will focus on, the next step will be to find out whether there are any affiliate programs for this topic, and if there are any products to promote at all. The niche you have chosen should have enough of the products and affiliate programs for you to start a moneymaking venture with. Otherwise it will not be worth your while at all.

As you research different affiliate programs, you should be aware of the types of merchants or brands using a certain program or affiliate network. One key thing to look for is other similar sellers who are also connected or using the network, as this will indicate the likelihood of success you will find with a specific program.

You should also know how much commission fees are being offered for lead and sales generations for the products being sold. For instance, if you will be utilizing ClickBank, products should provide at least a 50% commission and with a high gravity rating (indicating customer demand). For cost-per-action programs, commissions should at least be greater than $1 and offer you greater flexibility as far as promotional strategies.

When you research different affiliate programs, think about whether you would want to be associated with these products and services overall. Do the products being offered have excellent quality and relevance to your audience? Is there transparency in their manufacturing or quality control procedures? Are the retailers or companies of good reputation? Remember, as an affiliate marketer, any positive or negative view of the retailer will also affect your enterprise.

TheBalance.com's Duermeyer reiterates that entrepreneurs should select only the highest quality affiliate products and services. What you may want to do is buying the products yourself so you can judge their quality. Your audience will judge you based on the products or services you are promoting, so don't just look at potential earnings but also on the quality of what you are promoting

Be aware of the level of customer support provided by the program. Do they offer support via telephone, Skype, e-mail, chat, or other channels? How fast is the average response time? If you are able, contact other affiliate marketers already in the program so you can find out how good their customer support is. This is very important because sooner or later, you will need some support for your affiliate marketing efforts, and how they handle your queries or issues would be critical.

After you have done your research on possible niches and affiliate programs, the next step would be to set up your website. Most retailers will want to look at your website before agreeing to any affiliate marketing partnership with you; additionally, most networks also look at the website to make sure that the content of the site will not hurt or damage the reputation of the company or the brand.

If this is the first time you will be building a website, the great thing to know is that there are plenty of options available for beginners nowadays. Building a website has become a more straightforward, more user-friendly process. One of the easiest options you can consider is WordPress. WordPress has a CMS and user interface that is easy to learn, simple to use, and with many additional tools or features to make the experience more convenient for you and the viewer.

For those who already have some experience with HTML coding and other basics of building a website, there are more advanced options also within WordPress to add customization to the website. However, users with little to no knowledge of coding will find that the simple interface and features of WordPress make site building an easy task that should not take lots of hours to learn and master. For instance, you will find dozens of different themes within WordPress which will let you design a theme that is appropriate for your website. You can do this without having to change any code. There are free WordPress themes, and you may also invest in premium WordPress themes for minimal fees.

WordPress also features plugins which allow users to add different functionalities to their websites or blogs. Currently, there are over 50,000 plugins compatible with WordPress, with each plugin boasting of customized functions catering to the needs of different websites and their viewers, ranging from payment processing, search, subscription trackers, site visitor trackers, and more. Some third-party providers also offer free and paid plugin packages which are compatible with WordPress.

Of course, there are other options available if you would like to explore other options aside from WordPress. Regardless of what you decide to do as far as web hosting, you will need to purchase a domain for your website. The domain is the web address for your site, and you should have more than one domain names in mind. Remember that there are millions of websites currently published on the Internet, so it is entirely possible that the domain name you are thinking of may already be registered by someone else. This is especially true if the topic or niche you have selected is quite popular.

One of the most popular options for domain purchasing services is GoDaddy. This Internet domain registrar and Web hosting firm is publicly traded and headquartered in the United States. With over 17 million customers across the world and more than 6,000 employees situated in various locations, GoDaddy is considered the largest web host based on market share.

Another well-known option for domain name registration is Namecheap. Aside from domain name registration, Namecheap, which is based in the United States, also offers web hosting services. Namecheap was launched in 2000 by Richard Kirkendall. By November of 2010, a Lifehacker survey named Namecheap as the best domain name registrar. It was also appointed "Most Popular Domain Name Registrar" in polls conducted by Lifehacker in 2012. Namecheap has about three million customers and manages around seven million domain names on the Web.

After you have purchased your domain name or web address, you will need to set up the web hosting. Web hosting refers to a location on the Internet where your website files will be stored. There are many trusted and cost-effective web hosting providers on the Web today, including GoDaddy and Namecheap which were already mentioned above. Other well-known hosting providers include HostGator and BlueHost.

There are both free and paid web hosting service providers you will find on the Internet. Free hosting services, however, are not as recommended for businesses, let alone an affiliate marketing business such as the one you are looking to build. Remember, for your audience or site visitors to be able to access your website and its content, your website must be hosted somewhere. Some of the free hosting providers are not as reliable or insert their own advertisements, pop-up ads, and other content that may slow down your site's loading time or distract the attention of your viewers. In this regard, a paid hosting service is more advantageous for you as an affiliate marketer.

When you consider different web hosting providers, look at the most critical factors such as their uptime or reliability (the percentage showing the time that their servers are up and running); customer support options (phone, chat, email, availabilities, average response times, etc.); storage and bandwidth limits offered; costs and packages (Linux-based hosting services are generally cheaper than Windows-based hosting); and other features provided. You would also want to research whether the company is offering shared hosting (meaning you will share the server with other websites) or dedicated server hosting (compartmentalized into virtual servers, usually more expensive).

When your website hosting is up and running, the next step is to install your content management system or CMS. If you are using WordPress, this process is straightforward and self-explanatory, and you should have the installation done within a few minutes. Majority of web hosting providers offer simple installation options for WordPress users.

Once installed, you can then start to customize your website starting with the theme. As already mentioned, WordPress has many different themes you can choose from, each with customizable settings so you can tailor-fit your site's look and feel.

When your website is ready, you can now begin creating content and start marketing the products. But first, you will have to officially join an affiliate program that is related to the topic or niche you have eventually selected. The content you will be creating, as well as the marketing techniques you will be utilizing, should revolve around the products you are looking to market to your audience.

In the next chapter, let us take a closer look at some of the affiliate programs that entrepreneurs today are working with.

Chapter Summary

- Affiliate marketing requires commitment, patience, and hard work like any other business enterprise.

- An affiliate marketing business requires a specific niche or market.

- There may be more than one affiliate programs for a specific niche, so it is important to do your research.

- Different affiliate networks offer varying commission fees and payment tiers.

- For beginners, WordPress is the most recommended option for website building.

- You will also need to purchase a domain through a provider such as GoDaddy.

- Reliable web hosting is important for your website to remain accessible.

Chapter Three: Different Affiliate Programs

A simple Web search for affiliate marketing programs will yield many results, with various programs for small- and medium-sized websites and blogs all offering their own benefits and features. Before you decide on an affiliate program, you would want to know as much as you possibly can about the program. This may include the type of products or brands they offer, costs or fees associated, what commission fees or percentages they provide to affiliates, and other essential information that would be crucial to your success in the Web-based affiliate marketing venture.

The good news is that affiliate marketing programs make the process relatively easier for entrepreneurs, bloggers, site owners, and other interested parties who otherwise may find it more difficult or intimidating to contact big-name brands and retailers about possible partnerships directly. Also, in affiliate marketing, affiliates are not required to offer their own products or services. Instead, the focus is on promoting other merchants' products on their sites and online channels, providing a way to generate revenue without necessarily offering an in-house product.

Affiliate marketing programs usually require the merchant to oversee logistics such as actual transactions or sales of products and services, processing of customer orders, and shipping the products (many merchants also utilize networks for this part of the process). What you, as the affiliate marketer, will be handling is the promotion and lead generation, while in return collecting a commission for every sale or lead you deliver to the merchant.

LinkShare. One of the most popular affiliate programs in the world today is LinkShare. It was founded by Stephen Messer and Heidi Messer in 1996, and aside from its New York City headquarters, the company has offices in London, Tokyo, San Francisco, Tampa, and Chicago. LinkShare has over 10 million affiliate partnerships, and it is reportedly the largest affiliate network today. LinkShare held the top spot in the 2012 Blue Book of Top 20 Affiliate Networks, boosted by its platform strength, international capabilities, and support quality.

In 2005, Japanese shopping portal Rakuten, Inc. acquired LinkShare for $425 million. The deal enabled Rakuten to enter the lucrative U.S. market, as LinkShare had ongoing partnerships with major clients such as Apple Computer Inc., Lands' End Inc., Match.com, Delta Air Lines, Office Depot Inc., Orbitz LLC, and Wal-Mart Stores, Inc.

A report on the deal which was published in *The Star* noted, "Japan's largest online shopping mall operator said that it would purchase all shares in the New York-based LinkShare from its founder and others. The news helped push up Rakuten shares on hopes for the new business opportunity. In trading on the Jasdaq market, the stock rose 0.7 percent to 89,400-yen (US$818; euro652) midday after hitting an intraday high of 92,000 yen

(US$842; euro672). The planned purchase of the U.S. company roughly valued at 46 billion yen in the Japanese currency is the largest for Rakuten ... Before that, its largest acquisition was the 32-billion-yen purchase of Mytrip Net Co. in 2003, Japan's biggest accommodation reservation Web site operator, which is currently Rakuten Travel."

LinkShare has over 2,500 different affiliate programs. Users can choose to have LinkShare control each step of the affiliate channel management, or manage their own program and only utilize the service and support options provided by LinkShare.

Commission Junction. Another large affiliate program is Commission Junction. This is the largest affiliate marketing network in North America today and holds the number two position in the 2012 Blue Book of Top 20 Affiliate Networks, having been cited as "best at balancing the relationship between the merchants, the network, and the affiliates." Commission Junction is owned by Alliance Data and has operations all over the world. It is headquartered in Santa Barbara, California, and maintains offices in Atlanta, New York, Chicago, Germany, France, Sweden, Spain, South Africa, and the United Kingdom.

Commission Junction provides a host of affiliate, tracking, and media services for entrepreneurs, and allows users both self-managed and company-managed options for affiliate marketing. Commission Junction has a pay-per-action affiliate program as well as a PayPerCall program which assists affiliates in ensuring that they are earning commission for generated leads, making ad placements more profitable and encouraging the expansion of promotional online and offline efforts.

ShareASale. Cited as the "overall best performance marketing network in the world today" in the 2012 Blue Book of Top 20 Affiliate Networks, ShareASale, based in Chicago, offers over 2,500 various merchant programs and partnerships with well-known brands such as PS Pring and HootSuite. ShareASale assists in finding products to promote, while allowing affiliates to utilize their own websites or blogs, set up PPC or SEO campaigns, and employ RSS and email aside from other online means.

ShareASale was launched in 2000 by Brian Littleton and is currently among the top affiliate networks in the United States as far as the number of advertisers using an affiliate network. It has over 700,000 affiliates, over 86% of whom are members of the network. The company is known for its excellent ratings in ethics, customer service, reputation, security, and ease of commission payment practices.

Amazon Associates. Another large and diverse affiliate program is Amazon Associates, with an extensive range of products and services that would be sure to match with almost any category or niche you may be thinking of. The 2012 Blue Book of Top 20 Affiliate Networks placed Amazon Associates in the fourth spot, citing its stellar reporting system that exceeds other big networks.

Amazon Associates is a pay-per-sale affiliate program offering over a million different products which you can promote on your website or blog. Many small- and medium-sized websites and bloggers have benefitted greatly from Amazon Associates' affiliate system, as reported by *TheVerge.com*'s Russell Brandom in a February 28, 2017 article. Many publications such as *The Wirecutter* have been able to build thriving businesses around the model of affiliate payments, which pay out earnings and commissions to vendors like Amazon whenever a referred customer purchases a product. Brandom says, "Though some companies offer similar programs, Amazon's affiliate system is the most lucrative, and auto-tagged product links have become a significant part of many online businesses' revenue."

ClixGalore. An affiliate network based in Australia is ClixGalore. This program also maintains offices in the United Kingdom, United States, and Japan, and offers programs for affiliate marketers ranging from pay-per-impression (PPM), pay-per-lead (PPL), pay-per-click (PPC), and pay-per-sale (PPS). ClixGalore boasts of a two-tier network which allows affiliates who refer other affiliates to the network to also receive additional earnings.

ClixGalore has a solid network structure and offers thousands of different merchant programs across niches. Some popular international brands that have partnered with ClixGalore for their affiliate programs include Time Life, Citibank, Fox Sports Shop, Trend Micro, and Bluehost.

PeerFly. A pay-per-action network that manages its very own proprietary software system is PeerFly. According to the 2012 Blue Book of Top 20 Affiliate Networks, PeerFly had great staff, high popularity, and a top-notch platform, along with employees that were courteous, helpful, and willing to assist you towards the right direction.

PeerFly has a few thousand merchant programs to choose from, and more than 75,000 active publishers in 165 different countries. Some of the popular brands that have affiliate programs with PeerFly include McAfee, Uber, Target, CBS, LootCrate, World of Tannks, Beyond.com, LifeLock, Fiverr, ITPro.TV, Agoda, Booking.com, InboxPays, GameFly, IMVU, and much more.

ClickBank. Perhaps one of the most well-known of the affiliate marketing programs is ClickBank. This private Internet retailer was launched in 1998 by Tim and Eileen Barber and is a subsidiary of Idaho-based private technology firm Keynetics Inc. ClickBank itself is headquartered in Boise, Idaho, with additional offices in Broomfield Colorado.

As of 2014, ClickBank had over six million clients globally in 190 nations. It is known for its simple, user-friendly platform for businesses and entrepreneurs, and a wide range of digital products such as software programs, e-books, and membership websites. This affiliate program has been known to offer up to 75% commissions to many of its products. Commissions are sent out weekly, and direct deposit is offered.

In 2014, ClickBank CEO Matt Hulett said theirs is a "part payments company and part marketing company for entrepreneurs." By 2014, up to 30,000 transactions were being handled every day by ClickBank. ClickBank services include payment systems, tax calculations, and customer support options, apart from the affiliate network and marketing services for entrepreneurs.

MaxBounty. MaxBounty is an affiliate network that placed number six in the 2012 Blue Book of Top 20 CPA Networks. It was launched in 2004 and is known for higher payouts for affiliates, with commissions paid weekly. MaxBounty is based in Canada, and currently, has over 20,000 affiliates and 2,000 affiliate offers.

Some well-known brands and companies with affiliate programs through MaxBounty include Avon, Kroger, Acceptance Auto Loan, Avira, McAfee, PCKeeper, LootCrate, Kobo e-Books, Cash Crate, Fiverr, Amazon Prime UK, Uber, GameFly, CashUSA, Booking.com, Qatar Airways, Airbnb Host, Travofy.com, and many more.

Neverblue. The pay-per-action affiliate program Neverblue took the top spot in the 2012 Blue Book of Top 20 CPA Networks. The program rewards affiliates for performance in lead generation, downloads, and sales, and additionally for affiliate referrals to the program. In July of 2015, Neverblue merged with its parent brand, GlobalWide Media.

The acquisition of Neverblue by GlobalWide Media was completed in a $40 million deal in 2013 which included Neverblue and the AKMG affiliate network. Neverblue continued to operate under its Neverblue Media brand, while AKMG was merged with GlobalWide Media. Eventually, Neverblue was also rebranded to GlobalWide.

According to Farshad Fardad, Chief Executive Officer of GlobalWide Media, their top goal is the delivery of highly targeted profitable customers to their advertisers while also widening the scope of availability of other branded campaigns to their publishing partners.

Some well-known brands that have worked with GlobalWide Media and Neverblue include Jumia, AliExpress, Groupon, Hotels.com, MindSpark, Limango, and more.

Escalate Network. An affiliate and niche advertising network which targets mostly women audiences is Escalate Network. The Escalate Network has a 75% female network in the 25-44 age range and is a top performance ad network that mostly partners with family-friendly brands, retailers, and blogs.

Escalate Network focuses mostly on deal and coupon related offers online, encompassing coupons, samples, free giveaways, daily deal sites, cash back programs, reward programs, and other top-performing offers. Affiliates are paid via PayPal or check, and there are no additional fees for payment processing.

AvantLink. AvantLink is another leader in cost-per-sale tracking and solutions for affiliate marketing entrepreneurs. The network was launched in 2006 by Scott Kalbach, who emphasized innovation, quality, and service. As a cost-per-sale affiliate network, affiliates earn commission from sales, and commissions average about 10%. AvantLink also has other incentives based on performance.

Some brands that have partnered with AvantLink include Motorcycle Superstore, UnderArmour, Fanatics.com, Blendtec, Active Junky, Shop.com, 1800 Nutrition, AcuRite, BeautyTrends.com, BodyLab, CampGear.com, Coleman, Christmas Central, Duckworth, Duluth Trading Company, eParks, Drury University, CompexUSA.com, GearHut.com, Gordon State College, KEEN Footwear, Jans, Idaho Mountain Touring, Outland USA, ProBoardShop.com, PlanetGear.com, and The Good Ride.

Avangate. Avangate is a worldwide affiliate network for digital products and services. It boasts of a database of over 22,000 different software products and is backed by advanced marketing systems and commission rates that are higher than the industry standard. Aside from affiliate marketing solutions, Avangate is an all-around online commerce provider offering systems for subscription billing and global payments.

Companies specializing in SaaS, software products, and online services are the primary partners of Avangate. Currently, about 4,000 digital business located across the globe partner with Avangate for a wide range of e-commerce services, including Bitdefender, Brocade, Absolute Software,

FICO, HP Software, Kaspersky Lab, and much more.

FlexOffers. FlexOffers is an affiliate marketing network with advanced solutions geared to both publishers and advertisers. FlexOffers has a wide range of marketing options, data delivery solutions, payment systems, and a growing list of affiliate programs currently numbering about 10,000. The company specializes in lead generation, cost-per-lead marketing, cost-per-sale marketing, cost-per-acquisition marketing, and overall Web marketing techniques.

Some well-known brands partnered with FlexOffers include TruckProUSA, Hotwire, Priceline.com, InterContinental Hotels, Skechers, DirecTV, TimeLife.com, Cheryl's, The Popcorn Factory, Kohl's, 1-800-Baskets, Macy's, eHarmony.com, DentalPlans.com, SmartBargains.com, Soccer.com, Lenovo USA, GameStop, CreditSesame, P90x, Shake Weight, and Walmart.com.

eBay Partner Network. The eBay Partner Network is the in-house affiliate program of eBay. The network provides publishers various strategies for monetizing websites, blogs, social media pages, mobile applications, and other Web-based platforms. eBay Partner Network has become a leading affiliate program because of the large, diverse inventory, worldwide brand recognition, and higher conversion rates.

The program has the unique advantage of a large, worldwide audience. eBay currently has about 171 million active shoppers, and operations offices in 13 different countries. eBay has 5 million selling partners generating close to $70 billion in gross merchandise every year.

RevenueWire. RevenueWire is an affiliate marketing firm with an e-commerce platform that is designed primarily for online businesses offering software programs and digital products. It was launched in 2007 and is headquartered in Victoria, Canada. One of the key offers of RevenueWire is SafeCart, a shopping cart system that generates online sales and transactions in different languages and international currencies.

Some top brands working with RevenueWire include Adidas, KromTech, SOS Online Backup, Reimage, Avanquest, Comodo, IOBit, Pareto Logic, Spin Academy, and more.

ReviMedia. ReviMedia has advertising campaigns targeting both US and international markets, and an online lead generation platform with campaigns focused on insurance, home services, and financial services. The company has a proprietary platform called PX which is used for advanced lead generation and exchange. ReviMedia has a suite of tools for lead verification, scoring, and tracking.

Based in New York and founded in 2010, some client partners of ReviMedia include ADT, Alliance Security, Guardian Protection Services, Frontpoint, Vivint, Protect America, Moni, and several owned-and-operated brands such as BestQuotes.com, LoansOnline, MedicalAlertQuotes.com, MortgageOnline.com,

RefinanceCalculator.com, PetPremium, SecuritySystemQuotes.com, TopSolar.com, and HomeRenovation.com.

There are many other affiliate marketing programs you can explore. Every affiliate network has its own advantages and disadvantages, so it is a good idea to learn as much as you can about the different affiliate networks geared towards the niche you selected. But what are some guidelines you can follow when choosing an affiliate program? In the next chapter, let us look at some helpful hints when selecting the right program for you.

Chapter Summary

- Some of the most popular affiliate programs include LinkShare, ClickBank, Commission Junction, ShareASale, Amazon Associates, ClixGalore, PeerFly, MaxBounty, Neverblue, AvantLink, eBay Partner Network, and FlexOffers.

- Specialized affiliate networks include Escalate Network (geared mostly to female audiences), ReviMedia (campaigns for insurance, home and financial services), RevenueWire (software programs and digital products), and Avangate (digital products and services).

Chapter Four: Choosing The Right Affiliate Program

A huge component of your online affiliate marketing success hinges on choosing the most appropriate affiliate program or programs for your venture. Keep in mind that you will be creating content and coming up with various marketing and promotion techniques around the products and/or brands you eventually select for affiliate marketing, so pinpointing the right program for your website and other online platforms starts your efforts on the right path.

First, let us take a look at some of the different terms you will usually find referring to affiliate networks. A very common online advertising pricing model is the cost per acquisition or (CPA). Also referred to as Cost Per Action, Pay Per Acquisition or Cost Per Conversion, this model charges the advertiser when a predetermined acquisition or transaction takes place, such as a form submission, sale, click, registration, contact request, etc.

In the Pay Per Lead (PPL) form of CPA, fees are charged to the advertiser when the marketer can deliver a lead. For instance, when a user viewing your website or blog is directed to the website of the merchant, a percentage fee is paid to you. When a contact form submission or request form is filled out, you will also get a portion of the earnings.

Also under CPA is Pay Per Click (PPC) and Cost Per Click (CPC). In this form, each tie a text or display ad is clicked by a user, the advertiser is charged and will pay the marketer. Also related to this is Pay Per Download or PPD, where the advertiser is charged each time users download a specified file.

Experts in affiliate marketing generally suggest these guidelines as you choose which affiliate program is best for your enterprise:

Promote products that are related to your website or blog. The most important consideration is selecting products or services that go well with the niche, theme, or topic of your website or blog. Readers will have an easier time identifying the relationship of the products to your theme or niche if there is a conscious effort to market products that are at least in the same category.

If you are well-versed in the area of automotive accessories, for instance, and you have decided that this will be your site's niche, you would want to look for products, services, and brands that are related to automotive accessories and parts. Many of the larger affiliate networks would have specific categories related car parts, car accessories, and other automotive-related topics. Other niche affiliate networks, on the other hand, may not offer anything related to this category, so it is important to do your research.

Market products with positive reputation or acceptance. No matter how earnestly you attempt to promote a product or service, if the brand or the product itself is viewed negatively by the market, or has bad reviews, it will have a harmful effect on your website, and will also affect conversions. Keep in mind that one of your goals as an affiliate marketer is to appear as an authority or trusted reviewer of the products and services on your site. As such, you will want to avoid being associated with products or brand names that may damage the integrity and authority of your online platform.

It is very likely that when you choose an affiliate program to work with, you will have the opportunity to promote more than one brands, retailers, and product manufacturers. Remember that being associated with one negative product or brand can negatively impact other products or brands you are also promoting on your site, so it is crucial always to be aware of trends, reviews, and news which may have a direct or indirect impact on your conversions.

Use the products or services you are promoting. If at all possible, you would want to use the products or services you will be marketing online. This not only increases your authority as an expert on the products you are producing content about, but will also give you more ways to promote or talk about the product on your website, blog, and other online platforms. Some affiliate programs and networks allow you to try products for free before promoting them, while other programs give affiliates discounts on the products they are promoting.

Many online consumers and readers can tell if someone is genuinely familiar with a product or service or is merely promoting or writing about it without actually having had the chance to use it or become familiarized with it personally. To truly become an authority on the products you are promoting, look for ways to use them in your daily activities.

One helpful thing to do may be to make a list of products that you have owned or used in the past, or currently use, and then use this list to cross-reference with products and affiliate programs in networks you are considering. Any real experience you already have with these products or services will be helpful as you select which ones to promote and build content around.

After you have listed products which you already have first-hand experience with, you can pare down the list further by choosing those which you really love, have become loyal to, or use on a more frequent basis. These products would fall under your Expert Category, and from this list, you can choose affiliate programs being offered.

Look at the commission incentives of the program. Your primary goal in starting an online affiliate marketing enterprise is making money, of course. Your income from this venture will come from the commissions paid out by the affiliate network you will eventually join, so be sure you know the pay structure of the program and that you understand what this entails, including the possibility of increases and other incentives.

It is also important to note that some products or affiliate programs within a network or platform pay out higher or lower commission rates, so you should not assume that the rates are the same across the board for all the products. For instance, if you sign p with ClickBank, many of the programs offer a commission of at least 60 percent. Most of the products sold or marketed via ClickBank have an average retail price between $30 - $70, so you are looking at a commission of at least $18 per completed transaction. Some of the more established and popular brands have commission rates at even 75%.

While you would want to look at the commission rates, you should also consider the actual price of the product, and consider its affiliate program even if the commission rate is below 60 percent. For instance, if a big-ticket item retails at $160, even a 50% commission will give you an earning of $80 per sale, so it is still an excellent program to sign up for.

Another consideration is subscriptions or subscription-based products or services sold by the affiliate network. Even if the commission rate is at 50%, if you will continue to earn a commission each time the customer pays their subscription fee, then you are guaranteed continued income, and the lower commission rate is acceptable.

In this regard, you would want to consider Cost Per Acquisition (CPA) programs which pay out a commission for every monitored action instead of just each sale. Some CPA programs will reward the affiliate with a commission for lead generation or clicks, for instance, when the customer submits their email address or zip code or fills out an application form. NeverBlue, PeerFly, and Affiliate.com are some sites with CPA programs.

Zip code offers are easy CPA programs that allow you to earn a commission for every captured zip code. Your target, as the affiliate marketer, will be to come up with a website and corresponding content that would be interesting enough for site readers to want to provide their zip code in order to qualify for additional promos or information. Zip code offers do not require you to sell anything to earn a commission.

Check promotional materials for use. When exploring different affiliate programs, you should also look at promotional materials or techniques which will be provided to you, or you will be allowed to use. In the world of online marketing, you are competing with other marketers and retailers for the attention of the viewers, so you should have at your disposal a variety of marketing strategies and tactics which will help you deliver the message to your intended audience. Some popular methods of promotional materials used online include banners, newsletters, product reviews, viral publications, videos, and more.

SEO is another popular method used for promoting affiliate products. SEO or Search Engine Optimization refers to tactics used to improve the visibility of a website or page in search engines using organic, algorithmic, or natural search results. Many SEO campaigns can take months before any results can be seen, but the impact can be advantageous. Many affiliate programs have in-house SEO professionals who can assist you in setting up campaigns, or you can opt to outsource your SEO campaigns as well.

Online coupons are also a popular form of online promotion. Coupons have always been popular among shoppers who are looking for great deals and bargains, and as more and more consumers have turned to online shopping for purchases, it was only natural for online coupons and discount promos to follow suit. There are many coupon-type websites which specifically promote affiliate products across different categories.

Also, a useful promotional method, especially for e-commerce platforms, is incentive programs, loyalty or rewards points, or referral programs. Loyalty and rewards points seek to give incentives to customers who choose to transact with a business. For instance, accumulated rewards points may be exchanged for items, cash back, rebates, discounts, or other incentives.

Referral programs, meanwhile, encourage customers to tell their family members, friends, and other acquaintances or colleagues about the products and services of the business. In online shopping, much like traditional brick-and-mortar stores, word of mouth remains to be one of the most effective ways to spread awareness about your brand and connect with new customers. Referral programs capitalize on positive recommendations and feedback to further expand the target market and extend the customer base.

Good old-fashioned e-mail is still one of the most effective ways to get in touch with your target audience. Despite the popularity of online messaging apps, social networks, SMS, and other forms of online or Web-based communication, e-mail is still a surefire way to get the message across and interact with your existing, new, and potential customers. In affiliate marketing, one of the most common ways that e-mail is used for promotions is through newsletters. Some newsletters are sent daily, weekly, or monthly. Other marketers and retailers send out e-mail newsletter blasts whenever they have upcoming or ongoing promotions such as discounts or clearance sales.

Nathan Hangen, co-founder of Virtuous Giant, and creator of WordPress crowdfunding plugin Ignition Deck writes in a blog post for *Kissmetrics.com*, says that the times have changed and AOL no longer mails out CD's, but "we can still thank them for introducing us to email and our addiction to it." Hangen points out that nowadays, these messages have been replaced with tweets, likes, and Facebook updates, but for many people there is still a special importance given to email. "In fact, because of the noise that is social media, one could argue that the inbox has become our virtual dojo, our place of solitude amongst the chaos," Hangen says.

Of course, a highly visible segment of e-commerce marketing at the moment is social media. Undoubtedly, a large chunk of your target audience will likely be social media users, some more active than others. Affiliate marketers must be aware that any content or marketing efforts they publish on their website or blog should also be released on various social media platforms. Social media has a vast audience and holds a lot of potential as far as raising awareness about your brand's products and services, as well as connecting with audiences you may not be reaching through your website, blog, and other promotional materials.

Of course, central to the promotional efforts would be the website or blog where content would be primarily published. Your website or blog is where your content will appear, including related news articles, information, research, product reviews, and other online content which establish you as an authority and promote your affiliate products and services to your market.

For affiliate marketers, reviews continue to be a highly-used and very effective promotional method. Reviews are especially proven to work because many online shoppers look for product reviews and feedback before buying products, especially if it is the first time they are purchasing the item, or they do not know a lot about the brand or the product. When used effectively, product reviews can make you a trusted source of information for the shopper, while also converting to leads or sales, thereby adding to your commission.

Check the permissions or approval needed for product promotion. Some affiliate programs require different conditions or parameters before affiliates can market their products. For instance, some affiliate programs do not allow Facebook campaigns for promotion of their products or services. Some other programs restrict or prohibit email campaigns or the use of Google AdWords. If you already have plans or are using any promotional campaigns which will be prohibited by the affiliate network, it may be best to look for another one with no such restrictions.

Assess the market for the affiliate program. Part of your due diligence is scoping out as much of the market of the affiliate network as possible. This is important so you know what you are getting yourself into, what the general environment or competitive field is like, and what you should be prepared to face. As a general rule, if there are plenty of competing affiliates for primary search terms, this indicates a healthy, thriving market.

A simple Internet search on a primary search term for your market will let you know whether there is moderate to heavy competition from affiliates, which is indicated by a healthy amount of PPC advertisements. If you see many PPC ads, it is one indication of healthy competition, and also signals that this is a potentially lucrative market.

Of course, while it is good to see that there is ongoing competition on primary terms, you should also be able to see whether there is room to make a profit in the market. One tool you may want to use is WordTracker, which helps you to check the number of niche search terms related to the market. Ideally, a good market would mean many niche search terms with less competition. So you are looking for a market with a lot of affiliates, but niche search terms that will allow you to corner a segment of that market.

Ask the right questions. As you speak with different affiliate networks about their marketing programs and assess the right one for you to work with, remember to ask the important questions that will reveal to you how these affiliate marketing professionals can be a good fit for you. For instance, you may want to ask the program for a list of marketers and merchants who are finding the most success in their network. This will give you a general idea which niches are thriving and growing with the network.

As already mentioned briefly, some affiliate networks have very large, well-established product lines and categories that cut across niches, demographics, industries, and geographical locations. Other affiliate programs, on the other hand, choose to focus on specific segments of the market, such as technology, electronics, health and fitness, beauty and wellness, insurance, consumer loans, etc. You may not find as much success signing up with an affiliate network geared towards home improvement if your niche is music lessons. While there are certainly consumers who may very well be looking for both, the vast majority of the target audience will be looking for something else and may not be interested in what you have to offer.

You would also want to ask about the different kinds of offers that are relating to affiliates in their network. Understanding this will assist you in identifying the various pay-for-performance models that are finding most success and buzz in the network. Also, an important question related to this is identifying the types of affiliates and marketing methods within their network. If you are planning to use methods such as PPC or coupon codes, an affiliate network specializing in coupon and search marketing campaigns would be best suited for your venture.

You should also find out if there are more than one products which are available for marketing and promotion to the same market. This is optional but can be helpful if you can identify more than one good affiliate programs geared towards the market you are targeting. Having multiple products to promote also establishes you as a trusted authority in this category, and makes your website or blog more valuable to your readers.

In the next chapter, let us discuss more about one of the cornerstones of affiliate marketing which is website or blog content. How can you optimize the content in your website or blog in order to give value to your readers, establish yourself as an authority on this topic, and deliver conversions? We will look at some guidelines in the next few pages.

Chapter Summary

- There are different pricing models used in affiliate marketing, such as Cost Per Acquisition (CPA), Pay Per Click (PPC), Cost Per Click (CPC), Pay Per Lead (PPL), and Pay Per Download (PPD), among others.

- Affiliate marketers should choose products related to their website or blog, and high-quality products with positive reputation.

- It is helpful to personally use products or services you are promoting in order to be more believable in producing content.

- You should be aware what promotional materials you are allowed to use.

Chapter Five: Writing Content For Affiliate Marketing

Great website or blog content will keep your viewers interested and also encourage them to keep coming back for more. At the same time, good content will lead to more conversions and earnings for your affiliate marketing enterprise. This is why it is imperative to come up with original, high quality, online content that sets you apart from other sources and will deliver value to your site visitors.

Write from your own experience. If at all possible, write content taken from your personal truth. In the world of affiliate marketing, it is painfully obvious when someone attempts to produce content around a product that he or she has not personally tried, or does not believe in. Readers want to trust you and are looking to you for guidance, and it will come across as inauthentic if you attempt to write reviews or anecdotes about a product you have not personally tried, or try to promote a service even you do not subscribe to.

Julia McCoy, writing for *ExpressWriters.com*, suggests in her article "How to Write Content for Affiliate Marketing" that entrepreneurs should not pitch products they have not personally used or even like. More likely than not, your readers can tell exactly what is going on, and they will no longer look at you as a credible authority on the subject.

Instead, you can write about what you loved about a specific product, and tell your readers how the product has benefited your life, enhanced your outlook, or given you something new, interesting, or special to think about, McCoy says.

Place yourself in your reader's shoes. This will help you identify what content would be of practical value to your viewers. How can your post attract the audience's attention? If you understand the target audience and what they are interested in, what activities they are involved in, or what topics hold their curiosity, you can zero in on potential topics that would be of value to their daily lives.

Your content should revolve around your reader. While it is acceptable to write about your experiences about certain products or services or highlight why you love a certain brand, you should keep in mind that the content should revolve around the reader. The reader's needs, wants, goals, and interests should be at the center of the content, and your marketing efforts, and keeping the content reader-centric keeps them interested and feeling like they belong.

Honesty is a key to successful content creation. You should try to be as honest as you possibly can when writing about products or services, promoting brands, reviewing new items, or discussing promos or special deals. In this age of online connectivity, it has become very easy for a customer who feels duped or conned into a defective, subpar product due to dishonest reviews or recommendations to come back and expose the truth, thus creating a larger mess for the source to clean up.

Always be honest about the pitches that you create for the products you are marketing. There is no need to hide or lie about a product's shortcomings or weaknesses. You can highlight the strengths and advantages of products without covering up their disadvantages. This is especially important for products that relate to the health and personal safety of consumers. You have the responsibility to disclose important information, positive or otherwise, that can impact the well-being of your audience. Your readers will be more likely to appreciate you as an authority and become loyal followers if they know that you can always be trusted to tell the truth.

Make it natural. The average consumer who visits your website or blog is bombarded with hundreds of different advertisements, marketing pitches, commercials, and other promotional campaigns on a day-to-day basis. For your content to stand out, it should not feel like just another marketing ploy. Rather, you should make it your goal to produce content that looks and feels natural as if the reader is getting a personal recommendation from a close friend.

One way to achieve this is to incorporate your affiliate products into various anecdotes or stories in a fresh, natural way. McCoy adds in her article "How to Write Content for Affiliate Marketing" that weaving the products into everyday stories helps you in keeping your content fresh and will also be an effective tool for building rapport with your readers while also making the affiliate products more appealing and relatable to your readers.

McCoy also suggests incorporating the products in daily activities you share with readers. When your audience can see something in action, they associate with it much easier. McCoy says, "showcasing how you've used or enjoyed a product and building those mentions into your everyday content is a very compelling tactic."

Provide useful, relevant statistics. Many readers are looking for numerical data that can convince them to choose a certain product or service. Lori Wade, a freelance content writer for *Thriving Writer*, notes, "People love to check stats, and they will definitely check an article that promises them results of some study. Of course, the statistics that you choose should be related to the audience, and the audience should be interested in this data."

Be original. Search engines will highlight original, high-quality content, and their search algorithms have been mostly successful in weeding out unoriginal content designed to only boost rankings without much value to readers. As an affiliate marketer, you should avoid copying and pasting content from other sources without proper credit or citation.

Foster discussion with your readers. In your website or blog, it is recommended to have a comments section where readers can leave feedback, ask questions, or discuss with other readers. When your website has a lively comments forum, you can expect more direct interaction and engagement levels with your readers. It can also be a way to establish a relationship with your target audience.

Another advantage of allowing comments in your website content or blog posts is the SEO benefit. Whenever readers are leaving comments in your comment section, the page is updating, and most search engines like frequently updated pages, so this helps with your SEO ranking. One thing to remember is to moderate your comments section frequently. You may use a comment spam tool also to lessen the instances of spam comments.

Make your content easy to share via social media. Including different social sharing tools into your website or blog posts will make it easier for your reader to share particular content they find interesting or helpful on their own social media accounts. Once shared, your content will be exposed to a different audience altogether, and increase potential clicks and conversions as well. From the search engines' perspective, social sharing frequency indicates websites or brands that people are liking, sharing, and discussing in their own networks, adding to the legitimacy or authority of the source. Some social sharing providers you may want to look into are ShareThis.com and Com.

Pay attention to the length of your content. Hannah Evon, writing for *HigherVisibility.com*, points out that although search engines place a priority on content with quality substance, they will also consider the word count of a submitted post. While length is not always a true reflection of the quality of a post, you would want to go for posts that have between 250-600 words. Evon notes that high quality content will find better results than filler pieces with little actual value, but a balanced post, with high-quality content but also longer form, tends to yield better results. While there is no set word count or an ideal length for blog posts, content is much more important.

Evon also emphasizes that rather than focusing too much attention to length, you should view each piece of content as an individual resource, and maximize that post by delivering as much value to the audience.

Be aware of your spelling and grammar as well. Evon adds in her article "Blog Writing Best Practices for SEO", "Search engines pay close attention to spelling and grammar, as well as informed users." Many low-quality websites outsource their content writing tasks to content shops that are notorious for producing low-quality content full of wrong spelling and grammatical mistakes. This is actually one reason for the Google Panda Updates, which identifies and weeds out low-quality content. If you would like your site to be considered an authority it should have as few errors as possible.

Use different approaches. You would not want your affiliate marketing content to appear contrived or formulaic, so find ways to keep the content fresh and engaging to readers. Look for ideas that will deliver the message to your audience in different packaging for better variety and relatability.

McCoy of *ExpressWriters.com* says it is important to change it up every once in a while so you do not become a monotonous blogger people would not want to read. Also, trying new approaches every now and then will also help you reach out to new audiences while also highlighting your experiences with different products, goods, or services.

Find out what products your readers love. You can monitor this based on comments or social media shares, conversions, sales, and other measurable data. Remember that your goal in affiliate marketing is identifying what your market is interested in, and pointing them in the right direction so you can deliver conversions to retailers. You should strive to provide content regarding things or needs that will actually relate to the lives of your readers.

Consider other affiliate marketing strategies that are also related to content production. One such strategy that assists affiliate marketers in building assets and expanding the sustainability of the business is list building with paid traffic. This strategy is especially effective for niches or categories that rely heavily on e-mail marketing or newsletters. In list building, the primary goal is to funnel traffic to a landing page that is designed to attract the readers to sign up or opt-in to the newsletter. Effective and persuasive copy or samples are used to promote the content.

Brian Clark, the CEO of Rainmaker Digital and founder of *Copyblogger*, writes in his article "Three Killer Content Strategies for Building Affiliate Marketing Assets", that targeted traffic should preferably be channeled from search engine pay-per-click ads, but there are also other cost-effective advertising methods you can look into. List building revolves mostly around opt-in conversion rates and the value of each subscriber over a tie period. In this relationship, valuable content is of utmost importance. You're not going to get someone to give up their primary email address unless you promise and deliver valuable content in return. And your lifelong customer value will be lower if you don't maintain a good relationship with your list," according to Clark.

If you want list building to succeed as an affiliate marketing strategy, it is essential to find a healthy balance between solid online content and various affiliate offers. The content should have value to the readers but also lead seamlessly and naturally to product recommendations that lead to conversions.

In list building, it is also crucial to maintain a high-quality score for the landing page, as this will also help with your Google Adwords ranking. A high-quality score can be achieved by hosting your landing page on a domain that has a lot of original, high-quality content and also featuring many inbound links.

Another strategy for building assets is link building on keyword domains. Clark explains in his *Copyblogger.com* post that this is mostly an SEO strategy focusing on two important factors, namely, Google's current algorithm for exact-match keyword domains, and social media link attraction methods or link-baiting. The goal is to build up link equity and trust in the domain, after which you can attract search traffic for popular keyword phrases."

The first step in this process is investing in the most appropriate keyword-match domain, or an exact match keyword phrase that attracts traffic while also promoting a rewarding affiliate program. Next, there must be a strategy for easy collaboration or sharing on social media platforms, with many bookmarkable or share-friendly content.

Make it your goal to become an authority site. When you become a legitimate authority site, you can enjoy a sizable number of subscribers and see a lot of inbound search traffic without having to spend too much on expensive domain names or advertising campaigns. An authority site is primarily focused on building a real, recognizable brand, and maintaining a website that ranks very well in search engines. A well-created authority site is practically immune from algorithmic changes that may be implemented by the search engines from time to time.

How do you build an authority site? It may take some time, but what sets an authority site apart from the others is the consistency in delivering great content that people are looking for. Authority sites capture the market and deliver conversions by covering topics that people are looking for and pointing leads to lucrative affiliate programs. The primary strategy of a successful authority site is building a bridge between profitable products and services to desirable, high-demand topics being searched online.

It is important to prioritize buyers over subscribers if you do have to choose. "Sure, you want subscribers... and when you dish out great content on a regular basis, you'll have them. But when it comes to making money with affiliate marketing, what you need are buyers. People who won't even consider buying are not good for your business," according to Clark.

What about outsourcing? Many affiliate marketers are quick to concede that they are not experienced or skilled content writers. But of course, content is a core requirement of affiliate marketing ventures, so a trend that has become a big part of many e-commerce marketing campaigns is content outsourcing.

Affiliate marketers who have the additional resources may opt to outsource their website or blog content to freelance writers, agencies, or firms that specialize in coming up with original online content for a wide variety of clients. Many websites connect both marketers and writers, such as Upwork and Freelancer. The affiliate marketer or publisher will post an open project on the website, and freelance writers will then bid for the job. The marketer or publisher can then choose from the different bids, where writers will give their best price (i.e., how many articles for a set price, or how many dollars per article).

Many affiliate marketers have found content outsourcing to be a convenient and reliable solution, but outsourcing is generally a hit and miss method for getting content. Many freelance writers can contribute valuable content to your site and forge an ongoing long-term partnership with you, but there are many writers who may not also be qualified or who churn out low-quality work. As an affiliate marketer, you may have to try more than one freelance writers before finding one or more who can really provide the content you are looking for.

Aside from online writers, another option for outsourcing you may want to explore is local students in your community. If you live close to colleges or universities, you may be able to connect with students with top-notch writing skills. Many students are looking for additional sources of income while also honing their writing skills and adding to their portfolio and resume. One advantage of working with local students is the ability to meet with them in person and discuss the topic face-to-face. You can clearly convey what you are looking for, and they can ask clarificatory questions right there.

When looking for freelance writers, you may have to pay a little more for better quality content. Some writers with very low rates come from non-English speaking countries or do not have English as their first language, and are only looking to make a quick buck by churning out low-quality content in bulk. This will reflect poorly on your website or blog, especially if you are targeting a primarily English-speaking audience. Also, spelling and grammar significantly affect your search engine rankings, so if low-quality or poorly-written content end up in your online platforms, this hurts rather than helps your online affiliate marketing.

Instead of wasting time or money on cheap articles, opt for reliable writers who can deliver high-quality and valuable content. You may have to pay a little more for the service, but in the long run, this will be a better investment for your enterprise. Outsourcing is a viable option if you do not have the time or skills to write content on your own, but the people who write for your website or other online platforms should be in line with the voice, tone, and quality of your affiliate marketing venture.

Consider private label rights resources. Affiliate marketers can also look into private label rights (PLR) articles for website content. PLR articles are online articles that become your property once you have purchased them directly. Once bought, the author of the PLR articles relinquishes his rights to the finished content. This means you can edit the articles as you see fit, attach your name as the author of the articles, and post them on your blog, website, and other online platforms.

There are various means of procuring PLR content. Some affiliate marketers and publishers purchase a PLR membership from a number of PR sites. This membership gives them access to different authors, articles, and categories. There are also non-membership sites where affiliate marketers can buy individual packs or bulks of PLR articles. However this option can be more expensive per article. An additional option is online forums or groups where writers resell PLR packs.

One advantage of PLR articles is the generally higher quality of the content compared to other outsourcing websites. Some PLR websites also provide market research information together with their finished articles, so you can be assured that the topics have been chosen based on or revolving around keyword search volumes and other marketing-friendly parameters.

Many PLR membership sites emphasize that they do in-house market research, or require their writers and content producers to perform the research before producing articles. Some membership sites also advertise that all their writers are native English speakers, so you are assured of higher quality content when purchasing PLR articles from them. However, a disadvantage of PLR articles is the simple fact that they can be resold and reused any number of times across the Internet. You will have to edit the content heavily to avoid posting duplicate or closely similar content on your website.

As an affiliate marketer, what you can use PLR articles for is getting ideas for topics, and then practicing and honing your own skills in content writing. Because you will have to edit the content yourself, you may find that continually going through the articles and ensuring that they are ready for publishing on your website improves your writing skills, and eventually gives you the confidence to produce the content yourself.

Should you source content from article directories? There are online article directories where you can also source reviews, posts, and other online content. With article directories, you are allowed to post the content to your site as long as you do not make any changes to the article itself, and you credit the author by posting the author's bio box and any other links within the content.

Of course, the most obvious disadvantage to this method is the prohibition against making any changes to the content. You will have to make do with the article even if there are spelling or grammatical errors, or if there are parts that do not apply to your own affiliate marketing efforts. Also, because no changes are allowed, there is a significant possibility that the content will be exactly similar to competitors who may also be using the same content on their own website.

Also, since you are not allowed to remove any links within the author's bio box or in the article itself, it may inadvertently link to other blogs or sites that direct your readers away from yours and affect conversions. You are also not allowed to insert your own affiliate links to the content. Because of all of these disadvantages, sourcing from article directories is not recommended for affiliate marketing.

Beyond the content writing part, one aspect of affiliate marketing that has emerged in significance over the last few years is social media. Your target market is very likely to be reachable via social networking, so much of your affiliate marketing efforts must be designed to integrate with social media platforms seamlessly. In the next chapter, we will take a deeper look at strategies for maximizing your social media presence towards delivering conversions in affiliate marketing efforts.

Chapter Summary

- Producing great online content requires writing from personal experience, and placing yourself in the position of your audience.

- Readers gravitate towards honesty and sincerity, and can tell if you are being too sales-y or manipulative.

- Originality and share-ability make your content more palatable to readers.

- To maintain your rankings, check your spelling, grammar, and post length.

- Use variety and different strategies to break monotony.

- Outsourcing is a viable option, but ensure you are working with high quality writers who are a great fit for your enterprise.

Chapter Six: Maximizing Social Media For Affiliate Marketing

As of January 2017, the most popular social network in the world, Facebook, had over 1.8 billion active users. In the United States alone, Facebook was used by 89% of Internet users, followed by Instagram at 32%. Ironically, Facebook also owns Instagram. The most popular social network sites worldwide aside from Facebook and Instagram were WhatsApp, Facebook Messenger, QQ, WeChat, QZone, Twitter, Tumblr, Baidu Tieba, Snapchat, Skype, Viber, Sina Weibo, YY, Line, Pinterest, LinkedIn, BBM, Telegram, VKontakte, and Kakaotalk.

The global statistics related to social media use are truly staggering. As of 2017, of the 7.47 billion worldwide population, an estimated 3.77 billion or 50% were Internet users. 2.78 billion of the world's population, or about 37%, were active social media users. Additionally, there were 8.047 billion mobile subscriptions (more than the global population) and 2.54 billion active mobile social media users (or a penetration rate of 34%).

What does all of this data mean to you as the affiliate marketer? The reach and power of social media, and particularly mobile social networks should not be ignored. In fact, social media should be at the top of your priorities when planning ways to reach, connect, and engage with your target audience. More likely than not, your target market is on one or more social media platforms, and accessing these social networks on their smartphones and tablets, aside from desktop computers.

Hannah Evon, in the article "5 Golden Tips for Social Media Engagement" published on *HigherVisibility.com*, remarks that one of the most crucial tasks of digital marketers is bringing their brands to life. A major aspect of that responsibility is being personable and relatable, meaning someone whom the users can identify and engage with comfortably. This is where many online entrepreneurs find difficulty, in particular, the area of cultivating an honest, real, and engaging social media presence. According to Evon, "This is problematic because if social media is a key outlet and your presence on platforms is failing to engage users, the content and/or services you have to offer will likely be underutilized."

Planning your affiliate marketing venture's social media presence need not be tedious or worrisome. In fact, social media is designed to be user-friendly, and if you already use it quite frequently on a personal basis, it will be quite simple and rewarding. Social media is also cost-effective, with a large potential impact provided it is done correctly. Through consistency and thoughtful interaction, you can use social media to broaden the reach of your online platforms, increase brand following and conversions, and also discover new, exciting possibilities in affiliate marketing.

The fundamentals of social media marketing do not differ significantly from guidelines followed by brands using other strategies. This starts with a social media profile that is optimized towards your message and does not confuse or conflict with your brand. Consistency in message increases the official look and authority of your overall online presence, including social media presence. This is especially important because social media hinges a lot on sharing.

Before you dive into social media content creation and sharing, your strategy should be clearly and precisely hashed out first. You should have a clear idea who is in your social network, the users you want to reach, and how to appeal to the interests of your target audience. Developing a clear social media content strategy now will save your time and effort later.

Utilize different content software and tools. Social media sharing can be automated to some extent for convenience. Popular social media tools such as Hootsuite allow the affiliate marketer to create, plan, and schedule different social media posts. You can use tools like Hootsuite and others so you can share and re-share content, and avoid having to post the same content multiple times across social media platforms. Scheduling tools like Sprout Social and CoSchedule can also help you in managing post schedules and interacting with readers.

Templates are your best friend. There is no need to make your social media planning more difficult than it has to be. You can make it easier for you to produce social network content by designing templates for social sharing. Templates can save you a lot of time and effort while making the process more streamlined and easy to duplicate. Many social sharing tools and providers allow you to create and use templates that are appropriate for your audience and promote audience engagement.

Develop a messaging guideline. Combine the information you collate by knowing your audience's interests, and researching trends, patterns, and behavior from different platforms. A successful strategy for social media content sharing combines data showing both the interest level and the engagement of the users. Using a messaging guide will keep you on point, lessen the effort needed to come up with messaging styles that work, and also reduces sloppy, disconnected content.

Your messaging guideline should integrate answers to questions that your users are looking for. You would want to create mystery or bring up questions to attract the readers' curiosity, catering to users who want to know what is in it for them. Your guide should also give room for interesting quotes, statistics, or facts that tease, highlight, or point towards the main content piece.

Social media is most effective when it has the most impact within the shortest possible space. Brief, direct-to-the-point, straightforward content on social media is easier to share, discuss, and link to, so you want to give just the important details while keeping it short and sweet. Visuals, images, and other eye-catching pictures can help to drive the point home or garner the attention of your reader.

Different social media platforms demand customized messages. As you are aware of, there are some different social networks at the moment which are most popular with users in different geographic locations. Every social platform is different, seeking to offer a unique experience to its users. Because of this, your affiliate marketing campaigns should also be tailor-fit to the different social media platforms for added impact.

For instance, if you are posting on Facebook, the maximum length of a status update is 63,206 characters. Any post over 400 characters is automatically shortened or truncated so that an ideal post length would be about 40 characters. Meanwhile, on Twitter, the maximum tweet length is 140 characters. An ideal post length on this platform would be about 71-100 characters. When tweeting, you do have to keep in mind that a retweet removes about 24 characters, while links added to a tweet take out about 24 characters from the total.

Check out what your peers and competitors are doing on social media. You should have an idea what your competitors are doing as far as a social media presence. Of course, this does not mean copying exactly what the others are doing. Rather, this is more of an analysis of the strategies being employed by your competitors and seeing what level of success they are finding with these strategies. Some things you can monitor are their post frequency, style of messages, tone, promotional offers, and other methods and parameters for social sharing. This also opens your eyes to the right expectations as you try to reach your audience.

Try to be as personal as possible. Hannah Evon adds in her article "5 Golden Tips for Social

Media Engagement", when it comes to custom messaging, being personal and unique when creating content is vital to encouraging user engagement. You need to be enticing and personal with each single post, while looking for creative ways to get clicks or interactions. For instance, using questions, quotes, or some other interactive text with your posts are effective ways to increase engagement.

Be mindful of your word selection. The average social media user you are trying to interact with is exposed to hundreds of thousands of different messages on a daily basis. This makes your word selection very important for capturing your market's attention. Certain words or phrases, when selected and used correctly, may help your post become more attention-grabbing and cause your viewers to click and interact.

Keep an eye on the performance data of your social media strategies. The performance of your strategies will indicate whether they are working, and how you can make changes or add to your current strategies in order to get better results in the future. For instance, reviewing data from Google analytics will reveal to you what is clearly working, what is not delivering results, and what you can do to make your social media content more engaging to your viewers.

Be transparent especially when dealing with negative user feedback. One of the advantages of social media is the opportunity for affiliate marketers, retailers, and consumers to have direct interaction. Unfortunately, this also opens up the reality of negative feedback which is highly visible to the public and can be disseminated within a concise period. How an affiliate marketer handles negative user feedback will determine whether the audience sees the marketer as truly a trusted authority, or just another marketer out to get their buck.

Both positive and negative user feedback or engagement must be acknowledged and addressed. It is easy to respond to positive customer reviews, but it takes more character, self-control, and professionalism to engage negative user feedback properly, perhaps even turning it into something positive to your brand or affiliate platform.

Evon says in her *HigherVisibility.com* blog post, that when the interaction with a user takes a bad turn, ignoring it can be disastrous. Remember that each engagement, even the not-so-positive ones, may be used to your advantage. Use the negative attention to change the narrative and garner positive attention, while also showing readers your brand's unique ability to solve a problem. "It will show that there's a person behind the social profile who cares about their audience and is invested in bringing the brand to life," says Evon.

No need to jump right into promotional posts right away. If you really want to build a relationship or repartee with your target audience, do not worry too much about posting affiliate marketing offers or content right away. That can come in later. What you do want to focus on first is building a quality online platform and delivering consistent, high-quality content first.

If the first thing that your audience sees when they view your website or blog is a bunch of blatant promotional posts, you may lose the chance to gain their trust first or establish yourself as an authority before pitching products. Try to find a way to connect to your target market first and provide different content that is of value to your readers, and then start introducing the marketing content.

High-quality content may consist of different forms of online messages, such as blog posts, Facebook posts, e-mail newsletters, YouTube videos, infographics or charts, podcasts, and other types of online media platforms. The more compelling, rounded, and enjoyable your content is, the more likely it will be for your website or blog to gain a loyal following. Also, engaging content gets shared across social networks and increases your site's visibility, putting you in a much better position to start promoting affiliate products along the way.

Get your audience excited through high-quality offers, contests, campaigns, and other engaging activities that allow your readers to get involved in the action. Hannah Evon suggests a Thanksgiving-related social media campaign, for instance. "A 'give thanks' campaign is a great way to interact with them." Your brand can promote an image or social media post that expresses different things you are grateful for in connection to your brand or niche. You can then ask others to also participate and share what they are grateful for during this season.

The *HigherVisibility.com* writer adds that in these types of social media campaigns, users react and engage more with the sentimental value. Your goal is not necessarily to promote any specific products or get social media followers who may very well be future customers, but just relating to them on a personal, human level. The personalization of your brand will make you more relatable, and this has definite long-term effects as far as engagement and recall.

She also suggests a photo contest for your readers, such as a Fourth of July-themed competition for reader submissions, "but it can be recycled into just about any holiday or season." For instance, a photo competition is a quick and simple way to build your list of followers while also reaching potential customers. What you will need to do is create a post on your social media platforms that explains the rules of the photo competition, and then offer a variety of prizes for winners.

Evon adds, "For prizes, you can offer cash, gift cards, a free item, or anything else your brand has to offer. People jump at giveaways, and with all the shopper traffic the holidays generate it's a perfect time to host such a contest."

Create urgency through time-sensitive deals and offers. Examples of urgency include special offers that end at "midnight" or "while supplies last". You want to create a feeling of time sensitivity among your readers, so they decide to click or purchase now rather than miss out. Enticing offers and urgent deals can be effective in convincing shoppers who are still on the fence about checking out a product or buying it outright. If they can purchase the item at 15% off in the next

24 hours, it may be all the encouragement they need to go ahead with the order rather than thinking about it for the next couple of days.

Make sure you are reaching your audience on the right platform. Every social networking site has its own characteristics and type of audience. Your marketing efforts should be in line with the general behavior, interests, and demographics of people using each social media platform you are targeting. Twitter, for instance, was once regarded as just a mixing bowl of mindless blurbs but is now considered a source of information and discussion by netizens.

Ensure that your profiles and contact details are accurate and updated. Drew Hendricks, a contributor for *Inc.com,* says, "When customers or users are interested in learning more about your business, and what you have to offer, the first thing they'll do is type your name into Google. Whether you like it or not, your Facebook profile will be displayed in one of the first few search results. And because people are familiar with Facebook, that's one of the links they're more likely to click on. Keeping this in mind, you should incorporate links to your website and relevant sales pages. You should also verify that your contact information is correct and encourage users to reach out to you with a friendly and visible CTA."

Don't neglect your other social media profiles as well, reminds Hendricks. While you are updating your Facebook profile, it may also be helpful to direct some of your attention to your Twitter and LinkedIn pages. While these social networking platforms will not always garner as much traffic as

Facebook, they will also appear in search results, and you need to ensure that they complement your Facebook page.

Find a balance between landing pages and product listings. For most social media users, convenience and ease of access are essential to conversions. Hendricks explains, "Some businesses have great success with driving traffic from social media to landing pages and then to a product listing. However, the large majority of social users aren't interested in clicking through multiple pages to make a purchase. They've been trained to respond to quick and easy sales--not long checkout processes. That's why you should consider selling directly from your landing pages."

Consider different tools that let you set up shopping carts on the page itself, such as Spaces. There is also an advantage to offering more than one payment method. The more payment methods you are able to offer on your landing page (such as credit card, PayPal, bank transfer, Bitcoin, etc.), the higher your conversion rates will likely be, Hendricks writes in his *Inc.com* article "5 Ways to Use Social Media as a Sales Tool".

Always comply with advertising policies. Every social media platform has its own set of advertising policies. Facebook, in particular, is known for its strict advertising guidelines related to what content may or may not be featured on their site. Compliance is particularly important for affiliate marketers to remember, especially because many of the popular niches you may be working in are not compliant with Facebook guidelines. This makes setting up Facebook ads more challenging.

One of the guidelines on Facebook and some other social media platforms relates to images. The largest social networking site does not allow an ad that has more than 20% text on the image. Also, Facebook prohibits illegal products or services, tobacco products or tobacco paraphernalia, adult products or mature content, content deemed too shocking or sensational, images directly related to personal attributes (such as weight loss), false content or misleading claims, and other disruptive, low-quality content.

As far as language, Facebook and other social media sites will not approve ads with discriminatory language or depictions. The best way to make sure that any ads you want to submit to social media gets approval is to review their advertising policies and guidelines.

Copying and pasting from other sources without proper attribution should not be practiced on your own website or blog, and is definitely not allowed on social media platforms as well. These websites' compliance teams are routinely checking content for unoriginal or directly copied material. Multiple instances of plagiarism can result in your affiliate account being suspended by the site, so it is best to avoid this altogether. Come up with your own content and develop your creativity and writing skills.

One important reminder for affiliate marketers is to ensure that their social media pages do not look directly connected or affiliated with the official pages of the merchant or retailer. A workaround for this requirement is using a generic name for your site or landing pages. Also, avoid using the official logo of the brand or merchant in your profile picture (using the logo anywhere else in the landing page should be acceptable). It should be absolutely clear on your landing page that it is a review page rather than an official page of the retailer.

Level up your social media content. You are competing with so many other marketers and message senders in social networking platforms, so it is a must not just to stand out but to make a lasting impact. Optimize your social media content through the use of high-quality content, which is a combination of appropriate and highly relevant images, a Call to Action (so readers know what to do next), and carefully selected wording. Optimizing your social media presence also includes regularly updating your pages and staying relevant. You should be on the lookout for ways to relate relevant discussions or cultural happenings to your readers and engage them in the conversation.

Social networking sites can be an integral component of your affiliate marketing business. Through proper planning, strategic positioning, and consistency, you can leverage your social media presence towards higher conversion, user engagement, and a reliable following that will build your audience for long-term interaction.

Next, let us take a look at common mistakes that you should avoid if you want to have a successful affiliate marketing venture.

Chapter Summary

- Billions of people use social media all over the world, making it hard to ignore in affiliate marketing.

- There are different tools and content software affiliate marketers can use for scheduling content, managing posts, and interacting with readers.

- Templates and messaging guidelines make it easier for you to produce social media content.

- Customize your social media messages depending on the platform and audience.

- Word selection and relatibility are very important in social media.

- Avoid being too promotional right away.

- Use time-sensitive offers, deals, contests, and campaigns to get the audience involved.

- Comply with advertising guidelines.

Chapter Seven: Mistakes That Affiliate Marketers Should Avoid

If you have never done any marketing before, venturing into affiliate marketing can be overwhelming to start with. One effective way for you to find your way around the world of affiliate marketing is to learn from the experiences, failures, and successes of other affiliate marketers who have gone before you. Other affiliate marketers can impart valuable insights and suggestions that you would do well to heed as you take your first steps in this exciting journey.

Do you have family members, friends, work colleagues, and other acquaintances who have already been involved in affiliate marketing for some time? Networking with these affiliate marketers can point you in the right direction. They may even give you contacts or referrals to firms, specialists, or professionals who can help in various aspects of your affiliate marketing business.

What are some common mistakes that new affiliate marketers should watch out for? Here are some of them:

Do not forego an e-mail list. An e-mail list is a database of e-mail addresses provided by your readers and site visitors. Some marketers have the wrong perception that their business will always be able to sustain itself, so they neglect to build their e-mail list, opting instead to rely mostly on traffic from search engines. However, as has been proven countless times before, search engine traffic cannot be relied on for results all the time.

Search engines such as Google are always updating their search algorithms. If a major change happens, you may find your online business suddenly impacted heavily by a loss in search engine traffic. An online affiliate marketing business with an e-mail list will have a backup source of contacts, while an enterprise without one will suddenly find itself without much of any traffic.

Do not rely too much on search engine traffic. As just mentioned above, no matter how much traffic you are currently getting from search engines, it is still wise to have alternative sources of traffic to your site. An update to search algorithms can impact your site, but the impact can be lessened or mitigated if you have other ways to reach out to your audience.

Other ways to maintain your online presence include guest posting (writing content for other websites and linking back to yours), social media marketing, e-mail newsletters, etc.

Do not think of affiliate marketing as a get-rich-quick scheme. In fact, affiliate marketing is more of a long-term venture that will require your consistency, patience, and a constant desire to learn and improve. Any program that promises overnight riches from affiliate marketing is likely just out to make a quick buck off of you, so it is best to steer clear.

Affiliate marketing works like any other business venture, whether online or offline. You will need to invest time, resources, energy, and a lot of hard work to build it from the ground up. You will encounter difficulties along the way, and you will inevitably make some mistakes as well. How you succeed in affiliate marketing hinges heavily on how you manage obstacles and bounce back from failures.

Do not expect to see huge financial rewards right away. You may see some small gains now and then, but more than likely these are profits coming from efforts you put in place a while ago rather than some change you implemented fairly recently. It can take some time before you regularly see a steady stream of profits, so psych yourself up for a long-term commitment. That said, affiliate marketing has proven time and again to be a sustainable business model, so if you are patient and hardworking enough, you will be in the game long enough to see yourself become profitable.

Don't focus too much on sales. Now, affiliate marketing is a business venture, and you should always be assessing your strategies for increasing leads and sales. But affiliate marketing is unique in that you are trying to establish a level of rapport with your audience so that even when you are pitching a product or service, it does not look or feel like marketing at all.

Many affiliate marketers become too engrossed with selling products and services that they forget to establish credibility as an authority site. As a result, their online platform looks like a blatant promotional or marketing machine, and they lose out on many long-term opportunities to connect with the audience and leverage their position.

As an authority site, your primary goal as far as content is providing a helpful, valuable service to people. Although sales are important, they need not be the driving force behind your affiliate site. Remember, your role is to supplement the promotional campaigns and direct advertising already being implemented by the retailer or brand. If all your site is doing is mimicking the promotional efforts of the manufacturer, then you lose your credibility to your audience.

Your affiliate marketing strategy should be to help your audience by providing solutions to problems they have. The solutions may come in the form of products or services you are marketing, but the approach should not be too sales-y. The overuse of manipulation or persuasion causes you to lose your credibility to your target audience. You want to maintain their loyalty by being an honest and sincere voice that helps to answer their queries or solve their problems.

Avoid promoting too many products or services than you can handle. Try to keep the process as simple as you can, even with an online business such as affiliate marketing. There will always be the lure of adding more products and services to the list that you are already promoting, with the perception that this will lead to more money. This is not necessarily true, however, as you will often find that there is more money to be made when you focus on fewer affiliate products and services and maximize them.

If you have fewer products to promote, you can invest more time and effort in promoting them, and also focus on how to make these services or products relatable to the daily lives of your target market. On the other hand, if you have way too many affiliate products to handle, it can get overwhelming, and there is a tendency to neglect some of the products, thus preventing you from maximizing their potential.

Another downside to promoting too many different products or services is the confusion that it can cause to readers who visit your website or social media pages. Because there are way too many affiliates being mentioned, the message can get lost in translation, as opposed to a more streamlined, unified approach that is clear and concise to the average reader.

Never underestimate the power of keyword research. While you should not focus too heavily on search engine traffic, you should not ignore its impact also. In planning and strategizing your content for affiliate marketing, ample time and effort should be invested in proper keyword research. When done properly, keyword research makes your content more tailor-fit to the people you are trying to reach and increases your conversion also.

Keyword research is a tool that keeps you from getting sidetracked when producing content for your online platforms. It reminds you of the search terms that your audience is interested in, and helps you formulate a strategy that can relate to them personally. Keyword research also helps with rankings, and this is an essential aspect for affiliate marketers always to be mindful of. Keyword research does not take a lot of time and effort, but its benefits can greatly assist you in achieving your online affiliate marketing goals.

Your tracking and testing should be consistent. Andrew James of *BrandBuilders.io* explains, "A lot of affiliate marketers (too many, actually) do not track what is happening on their website, and make changes based on their emotions and feelings rather than what the data is actually telling them to do. Implementing basic tracking isn't difficult, especially if your website is built on WordPress."

James adds, "Installing the "Pretty Links" plugin is one of the easiest ways to see what links people are clicking on and allows you to verify that the clicks you're sending to the affiliate network are being properly tracked. Then, when you're ready to make changes to increase your conversion rates, you can split test and have data to back up the decisions you make. This is critical since most people make changes and have very little in the way of data to tell them if those changes were effective, and how effective they actually were."

Tracking clicks and conversions lessen the potential for wrong data from affiliate networks or inaccurate sales records. "As your business begins to grow, you can use more expensive methods to track what you're doing, what your visitors are clicking on, and which links (or website copy) is generating the most sales for you. Then, devoting more effort to the winning changes you've made will increase your income even further. Without tracking what's happening on your site, you're hoping and praying that you'll become successful, instead of knowing that you're doing the right things," James says.

Don't lose sight of your niche. Affiliate marketers with a hefty budget, lots of experience, and the technical skills may opt to take on the more significant players in the industry by expanding their focus to a broader topic. If you are still a beginner in affiliate marketing, however, it is best to fix your focus on a smaller niche within the industry where you can excel, hone your skills, and learn the ropes of the online business.

This is not to say that you should never dream big. Your goal should always be to improve, learn from your past experiences, and progress to bigger and better things over time. But this should not come at the expense of losing sight of the more important things. Your target should be to establish yourself first as an affiliate marketer with moderate success within your chosen niche or specialized category before attempting to compete in the broader topics or categories.

Eventually, if you start off on the right foot, even with just a tight niche, you will find your online presence growing, with higher traffic numbers, and you can diversify your content and affiliates so that you can make inroads into the larger segments of the industry. For now, however, it is best to start out smaller and focus on mastering the ins and outs of the industry first.

Copywriting is always integral to sales. You will not always be able to convert a lead on their very first time to view your website. More than likely, it will take several visits to your online platform before you can persuade them to become more than just a reader. What will keep them coming back? It is the quality of the copywriting in your content.

Brandbuilders.io's James notes, "Whether you're selling your products and services, an affiliate product, or selling people on the reason they need to sign up to your email list, your content does all of the heavy lifting for you. Learning how to write proper copy can take years, though."

He again stresses that you should focus your writing on solving your reader's problem rather than pitching a product to them. "The best way to write compelling copy is to get inside of your visitor's head, figure out the problems that they're having, and then get the same conversation into your content while showcasing that the product or service you're promoting is the solution to those problems. When you're able to get your visitor excited about solving a problem they're having, making sales is going to be substantially easier than simply writing content to sell a product."

Avoid overloading your site with too many links and ads. A page that has too many different ads for different products looks like it does not have a clear goal, and instead of being a sales funnel can actually drive your target audience away. Many affiliate marketers decide to load their website with too many ads and links to affiliate products because they think this opens the doors to more earning opportunities. While there may be short-term gains, the long-term results of overloading would have a greater impact.

A website with too many ads and links can give a confusing message to the reader, and instead of capturing their attention, you may end up frustrating the viewer who is really just looking for information. This can cause you to lose that reader. Instead of too many links and ads, have a clear goal for each page and come up with a unified strategy that makes it very obvious what you would like the reader to do next, such as subscribing to your e-mail newsletter or clicking on the sales page.

These are just some of the timeliest reminders that every new affiliate marketing entrepreneur should keep in mind. Many other experiences and lessons will be picked up along the way. As you grow and become more skilled in the intricacies of online affiliate marketing, remember the lessons you have imbibed along the way and use them to your advantage as you move on to higher levels of success.

In the next chapter, let us take a peek at popular trends in affiliate marketing which industry insiders are predicting would shape this segment of digital commerce over the next few years.

Chapter Summary

- Affiliate marketers must have an e-mail list rather than relying solely on search engine traffic.
- Affiliate marketing is not a get-rich-quick program; it requires hard work and strategy.
- Don't promote too many products or services. Keep it simple.
- Keyword research, and website tracking and testing are important parameters for affiliate marketing success.
- Don't overload your website with too many links or ads.

Chapter Eight: Trends In Affiliate Marketing

It is undoubtedly an exciting time to be involved in e-commerce. The industry is growing by leaps and bounds and continues on an upward trajectory. Online shopping and Web-based sales models are poised to revolutionize the future of consumer purchases and transactions, and if you are involved in this global revolution, you are in for a lot of exciting changes and fast-moving developments.

Affiliate marketing is not a new phenomenon in Internet marketing, by any chance. It sprung up as a basic component of Internet-based consumer marketing because of its simple, tested model mirroring other offline and traditional marketing methods. That said, affiliate programs are not all the same, and the most progressive and successful affiliate networks are always looking to improve the system, increase their efficiency, and become a more potent force in the overall industry.

In his article "Powerful Affiliate Marketing Trends in the Digital Economy" published on *TheBalance.com*, Brian Edmondson identifies three key trends in the affiliate marketing industry that are sure to cause changes across the board for the years to come. These include improvements in attribution roles, an increase in the role of mobile technology, and more partnerships with multinational and non-traditional players.

Regarding attribution, Edmondson concedes that both online and offline sales programs continuously have to combat deficiencies in attribution. "Imagine how affiliates feel when all their hard work to bring buyers to a website goes for naught. All it takes is a bad merchant credit system, "click-stealing" software, or other nefarious means." What this means is more and more companies will focus their attention on improving their compensation models and becoming more transparent in the coming years. This may include such strategies such as multi-touch, time-decay attribution, position-based attribution, and better data management in order to cultivate a fair, sustainable situation for all stakeholders.

Mobile technology continues to change the way e-commerce connects with and serves modern consumers, and affiliate marketing will also benefit from this trend. "It shouldn't come as a surprise that mobile technology will increasingly impact affiliate marketing for both the merchant and affiliate. In recent years, mobile commerce has been one of the strongest elements of e-commerce, thanks to the growth of traffic from hand-held devices like smartphones. Hence, the larger affiliate networks are reporting greater activity (traffic, sales) from wireless marketing efforts," Edmondson suggests.

Of course, those in the industry must also be prepared to position their online platforms towards mobile optimization in order to reap the rewards. "Affiliate programs must ensure that their websites and sales funnels are optimized for mobile. Otherwise, they risk leaving money on the table and losing customers to the mobile-friendlier competition. At a more psychological level, people are increasingly attracted to companies that offer a positive wireless experience," he reiterates.

With globalization and the increasingly interconnected nature of the modern marketplace, affiliate marketing will become more competitive on an international scale, even finding itself alongside non-traditional entities. Edmondson points out, "As more merchants come online to compete in various niches, companies will need "Out of the Box" thinking to find valuable customers. Going global is an increasingly viable option because even a small slice of the USD 1.5 trillion e-commerce marketplace justifies the hassles of international business (i.e., Compliance with national regulations, local customs, languages, scaling attribution rules, etc.)."

Even newer, small- to medium-sized marketers will benefit from the more level playing field of online commerce. "Smaller players may not have to change their digital marketing strategy drastically, but more established companies may want to enlist an independent agency or partners with international experience to ease the transition to global e-commerce," the article notes.

What does this mean for your online affiliate marketing plans? There will be exciting opportunities for growth and development if you are constantly on the lookout for ways to enhance the way you do business and how you interact with your target market. Gone are the days when affiliate marketing was considered a secondary business model. While it is still primarily a supplemental business channel, it has transitioned into a robust and reliable source for generating leads, sales, and ongoing conversions, especially when strategized correctly.

For the long-term benefits to be felt, affiliate marketers must have access to effective program management and improved reward structures for performance. Partnerships with high-value retailers and brands must not be neglected, but affiliate marketers must also find ways to incorporate those partnerships that enhance their branding and reach with their core followers.

There is a lot of room for growth especially as the affiliate marketing segment has matured in growth particularly in driving sales. In the United States, affiliate marketing spending is projected to increase by 10.1 percent between 2015 and 2020, ballooning to a $6.8 billion industry. At the moment, more than 80 percent of advertisers and 84 percent of publishers are running at least one affiliate program. Among advertisers, upwards of 80 percent have channeled more than 10 percent of their overall marketing budget to affiliate marketing. It is a segment that is continuing to increase in importance, and you will be right in the middle of this explosive growth.

Adam Weiss, the General Manager and Senior Vice President of Rakuten Affiliate Network, which is one of the leading players in the industry, says, "Affiliate marketing is a high-value, low-risk strategy proven to drive sales and awareness for brands and revenue for publishers. When done right, it cultivates mutually beneficial and authentic relationships between brands and publishers, and those publishers and their audience."

Chapter Summary

- The affiliate marketing industry is poised to grow bigger in revenue and influence.

- Attribution for sales will improve as affiliate marketing grows.

- Mobile technology innovations will continue to expand the reach of affiliate marketing efforts.

- Global entities and companies will look to further partnerships with affiliate networks.

Conclusion

Thanks again for taking the time to download this book, Affiliate Marketing: How To Make Money Online And Build Your Own $100,000+ Affiliate Marketing Online Business!

You should now have a good understanding of the affiliate marketing industry, including its primary characteristics, industry players, and how you will be able to penetrate this fast-growing segment of the digital commerce industry. As we have discussed, not only has affiliate marketing established its important role in the overall Web-based consumer shopping experience, but it has also proven its worth in identifying the preferences, needs, and purchasing behaviors of modern consumers, so businesses and retailers can improve their interaction with their market and solidify their position.

In the process, you as the online affiliate marketing entrepreneur will also have the opportunity to get your slice of the pie and establish a financially rewarding venture. All it takes is a passionate dedication to improving your craft and connecting on an interpersonal level with the people you are trying to reach, relating to them through carefully planned content and other strategies that position you as an authority and a trusted source of information and comparison.

If you enjoyed this book, please take the time to leave me a review on Amazon. I appreciate your honest feedback, and it helps me to continue producing high-quality books.

30670679R00053

Printed in Great Britain
by Amazon